Dan
Ro___ ___y

Written by Rozanne Lanczak Williams
Created by Sue Lewis
Illustrated by Patty Briles

Creative Teaching Press

Dan and Dot's Rainy Day
© 2002 Creative Teaching Press, Inc.
Written by Rozanne Lanczak Williams
Illustrated by Patty Briles
Project Manager: Sue Lewis
Project Director: Carolea Williams

Published in the United States of America by:
Creative Teaching Press, Inc.
P.O. Box 2723
Huntington Beach, CA 92647-0723

CTP 3240

Rain, rain, stay all day.
We can have fun anyway!

We can wear funny clothes
and put on a play!

We can bake a cake.

Here are things
that we can make.

We can play in our plane.

We can play in our train.

We can call our friends
and play a game.

Rain, rain, stay all day.
We can have fun anyway!

Create your own book!

Cut out book pages in the shape of rain-drops. Write about the fun things you like to do on a rainy day. Color your pictures with water-based markers. Spritz lightly with water from a spray bottle for a "watery" effect.

Words in *Dan and Dot's Rainy Day*

Long *a*	High-Frequency Words		Other
rainy			wear
rain	we	our	funny
train	can	all	clothes
stay	have		things
day	and		call
play	put		friends
anyway	on		fun
cake	a		our
make	here		Dan
bake	are		Dot's
plane	that		
game	in		